I0484187

START A BUSINESS

For The Military Entrepreneur

By PERTRINA, LLC

Published by PERTRINA, LLC

Copyright 2015 © PERTRINA, LLC

This book is dedicated to

Kevin Jeremiah

TABLE OF CONTENTS

The Service Member's Guide To Online Business

Introduction

Whether you are living in the barracks, in government housing, or in your own castle, you can work on your financial stability and independence by earning some extra income which might turn into a fulltime gig for you, should you decide to leave the service.

In this Chapter, you will learn just how easy it is to set-up an online business and run it all within the *comfort* of your living arrangement. Traditional rules apply as if operating a brick and mortar establishment. Remember most all businesses require permits/licenses for the industry they are in, so run that request slip by your chain of command just to be on the safe side.

Online Business

Establishing an online business for military personnel is a great way to sell *services* (consultancy, freelance writing, etc.) Take advantage of your unique location as easy access to the post office, free legal aid and banking are vital to the success and management of your online business. Service members with their own home can easily follow these simple steps if they desire to sell, market and advertise goods online.

All goods require a barcode for each item which you sell. To take the uncertainty and guess work out of the process apply for one at the GS1 website, which will allow you to sell your products to big box stores (Amazon, Walmart, etc.) Look for possibilities at your NEX or AAFES location.

Once you have figured out the structure of your business, you need a domain name. Many sites offer domains, but you will need one that offers online-shopping as this will be your store front. Check out (godaddy.com, wix.com, etc.) It will automatically search to see if the name you have chosen is readily available. If the name you want meets your approval, go ahead and signup to register.

Most popular web hosts allow you to design your own website, or pay them to design your website. If your IT department has someone with their own site designer business, go ahead and use their expertise. You will most likely get what you need for less or nothing. To create high quality images of the products and/or services you offer on your site, invest in a great digital camera. You don't have to be a professional photographer to take amazing pictures. Search videos on YouTube to learn how to make a light-box for product photography.

We all know that soliciting on government property is prohibited, so use your network connections to spread the word about your business in order to generate the customers you need for a successful business. You can do so through a variety of channels including social media (Facebook, Twitter, Instagram, Pinterest, etc.); but also register with search engines like (Bing, Google, etc.) to drive traffic to your website.

Make use of printed media to design and print (brochures, postcards, etc.) and have them delivered to your potential customers. Newspapers are a more traditional way of advertising, so be sure to take advantage of every avenue for advertising, provided that you will be reaching your **target market.**

Contact Base Legal to learn about internet law, as you must comply with the laws and regulations governing anticybersquatting, online selling and delivery of services; children's privacy protection guidelines as well as follow state and local laws.

If your online business is domestic and within the US, then you are responsible for collecting local taxes from customers and may need to apply for a tax permit from your state revenue agency. If stationed overseas, you will need to consider the international trade laws for your market, to be able to find suppliers, arrange international shipping and follow special tax regulations for the Country you are in.

The Veteran's Guide To Starting A Business

Introduction

This is a book for the military entrepreneur. It's a guide for any individual with a desire to demonstrate leadership by becoming their own boss and starting a business for themselves. Honestly though, for me, this book is a social experiment to see just how easy it is for a homeless, black, female, veteran and single mother; to pay off all her debt, purchase a home, and get back on her feet by becoming productive again to herself and her family.

So, I invite you through this year long journey with me as we explore the pros and the cons; the highs and the lows about starting a business. You will learn of what to expect, and the things to look out for before, during and after you start your business. I look forward to your feedback about how this book has helped you plan for this exciting and risky time in your life.

Starting my first business by age 31 would not have been remotely possible without the generous support of persons like you. By purchasing my books you are contributing to a cause, others like myself will benefit because of your support. Thank You! Your donations help us one step further to achieving the goals for this year and beyond.

Benefits

It has been my experience that 'Women –Owned', 'Veteran Owned'; as well as 'Minority-Owned' Businesses were designed to help these groups navigate through the procedures of starting a business, but looking at them under a microscope, these programs are simply for the most part- just smoke and mirrors. This basically boils down to following the steps outlined in this book that will help you to a smooth transition.

The first thing you should do when searching for financing is ask family/friends who are willing to invest in your business and give/loan you the money; second-check your own TSP. If you have a sizable amount invested you can easily loan yourself the money and repay in as little as 2.13% which allows you to set the terms for length of repayment.

Look for a great credit union, with which you have already established a good relationship. You want one that will offer you a loan for your startup, inventory financing and equipment purchases with no prepayment penalties. Furthermore, grants are an excellent way to get the additional funding you will need to grow your business. See if you are eligible!

Service Members within six (6) months of leaving the service have a huge advantage for accessing financing and should pursue these options even before enrollment in the mandatory Transition Assistance Program, so start planning one (1) year ahead.

Structure Your Business

In 2014, I accumulated a stack of rejection letters from jobs I had applied for; from Federal positions, Embassies, Hotels to Theme Parks. I tried many online sites (Indeed, Fiverr, Elance, etc.) all with little to no success.

A year before my debt crisis, I had an idea while putting a batch of cookies into the oven to bake one Sunday afternoon. My son loved snicker-doodle cookies and I had a bag of unopened coconut sitting in the pantry which I had no idea what to do with so instead of throwing away the soon expiring bag, I put it in the next batch of cookies I made. Soon my son was bouncing of the walls because as it turned out the cookies were way too sweet, I hadn't paid attention to the fact that the coconut was sweetened; but it reminded me of a 'sugar cake'.

Fast forward a year later and some tweaking of the recipe, I had my idea for a business with no clue as to where to start, who to ask, or even how much it would cost. I am happy to share with you today, the things I learned along the way. Doing what you love while making money from it is half the battle, knowing how to get your start-up off the ground on the other hand is stressful, but only for the first 15 minutes.

Don't be overwhelmed, little did I know I could start my own business within 24-48 hours. First, you should make a determination whether you are going at it alone, with business partners, etc. This step, simply put, is known as the 'business structure'.

Sole Proprietorship

In essence, sole proprietorships are popular among start-ups because they involve only one person-the owner. That individual has responsibility for all the profits and all losses, debts and liabilities. No formal action is required when forming a business with sole ownership.

Since there is no difference between you and the business, then the business is not taxed separately but rather the income of the business becomes your income and is reflected that way when the owner files taxes. Income and loses are reported with Schedule C and the Standard Form 1040. Also, the owner is responsible for the withholding and payment of all income taxes which include self-employment and estimated taxes.

The advantages of being a Sole Proprietor are as follows: it's relatively easy and inexpensive to set up; there is complete control for the owner to make all decisions; and there is easy tax preparation.

Alternatively, the disadvantages are: the owner has unlimited liability and is liable for the debts and obligations of the business; it's difficult to raise money as you can't sell stock-investors won't invest; and the owner has ultimate responsibility for the success/failure of the business.

Limited Liability Company

This structure, like the name suggests provides limited liability features of a corporation, and also the tax efficiencies as well as flexibilities of a partnership. Owners of a Limited Liability Company as considered 'members', who can be one or more individuals. LLC's are not taxed separately, but profits and losses pass through the business to the owner(s). The members/owners report profits and losses on their personal tax returns.

A Limited Liability Company becomes valid in 4 steps:

First, file the Articles of Organization.

Second, create an Operating Agreement

Third, obtain licenses and permits

Finally, advertise in your local paper to announce your business

All LLC's must file a sole proprietor, partnership, or corporation tax return. Certain LLC's automatically classify as a corporation by federal tax law. LLC's that are not automatically classified as a corporation can elect to do so via Form 8832. To make special election to be taxed as an S-Corp, use Form 2553. Single Member LLC file Form 1040 Schedule C; Partners of a LLC file Form 1065 Tax Return; LLC's filing as a Corporation file Form 1120.

The advantages of an LLC are as follows: If the LLC acquires debt, the member's personal assets are exempt. Members/owners are protected from personal liability; there is less registration paperwork and smaller start-up costs. There are few restrictions on profit sharing.

In comparison, the disadvantages of an LLC are: if a member leaves, the business is dissolved; members of an LLC are considered self-employed and therefore pay contributions towards Medicare and Social Security.

Cooperative

Any business or organization that is owned or operated for the interest of persons using its services is called a cooperative. Members/user-owners share in the distribution of profits and earnings. The cooperative is managed by an elected board of directors. Becoming a member is done through the purchasing of shares, but the amount of shares owned does not affect the value on the input of their vote.

To form a cooperative a group of members must first agree on a common need and ways to remedy it. Before the business plan is agreed upon, an organized committee meets and carries out surveys, research costs and conduct feasibility studies. For a cooperative to be incorporated, the following must happen:

*File Articles of Incorporation

*Establish Bylaws

*Introduce a Membership Application

*Elect Directors & Charter Member Meeting

*Seek permits and licenses

*Hire staff

The advantages of establishing a cooperative are that there is less taxation, more funding opportunities, costs are reduced as the business improves its good and services offered; there is less disruption and thus the business can continue; also there is a democratic process. Larger investors may be hard to find for a Cooperative business structure which may be a disadvantage of the entity. There may also be a lack of willingness for members to participate in the running of the business, with high risk of losing members.

Corporation

A corporation is owned by its shareholders and the corporation is liable for debts incurred. Administrative fees are usually higher and are have more complex tax requirements. Stock is offered at the corporation level, with becomes attractive to investors to raise capital when the business goes public (IPO).

When forming a corporation, it must first establish its business name or DBA name if doing business as a different name from the officially registered name. Once a corporation is established, then they must include Corporation, Incorporation or Limited at the end of the business name.

Some states may require a board of directors to be established and the issuance of certificates of stock to initial shareholders in order to begin the registration process. Articles of incorporation will also be required for filing in your State. As any business needs the necessary permits and licenses to legally operate, the same will be needed for this type of structure. State, Federal and even Local taxes are expected to be paid by Corporations, who must also register with the IRS.

Forming a corporation is indeed creating a separate tax-paying entity. Regular corporations/ C corporations adhere to Subchapter of Chapter 1 of IRS code, which are the general tax rules pertinent to corporations and their shareholders. Corporations pay income tax on their profits and must use Form 1120/1120-A to report revenues. Employees who may be shareholders also pay taxes on their wages. Both the corporation and employee pay Social Security and Medicare taxes.

Corporations are attractive because they can issue shares to investors; shareholders assets are protected and only accountable for their stock in the company. Double taxation is very possible on all profits and dividends. Another disadvantage to corporations is the meetings that must be held annually, and the minutes recorded. In addition, corporations are often costly and time consuming to form.

Partnership

A partnership is any business with at least 2 members. The partners share ownership and contribute to the running of the business in exchange for a share in the profits and losses. It is advisable to make a legal partnership agreement stating how the business will operate. The three (3) types of partnership are: General, Limited & Joint Ventures.

When forming a partnership, it is important to register first with your Secretary of State office. A business name will need to be established; for partnerships the legal name is the name on the partnership agreement, or the partners' last names. Operating under a different name than what was officially registered requires the filing of a fictitious name or "Doing Business As".

Partnership must then obtain the necessary licenses and permits for the industry, state and locality that they are in. Income, deductions, gains & losses are reported annually on the Partnership's Information Return; however the actually business doesn't pay income tax. The partners assume all profits and losses according to their share of the business.

The advantages of having a partnership are that they are usually not costly to start; the partners share in the financial responsibility as they have often pooled their resources to raise capital; there is specialized expertise that is acquired; and partnerships can offer potential employees the opportunity to become partner.

A major disadvantage to this business structure is the shared liability for debts and decisions of the partners as assets can be held by creditors to settle debt. All profits must be shared with the other partners, which can result in many disagreements because of unequal time or money invested by any partner.

S Corporation

A Corporation which makes a special tax election through the IRS using Form 2553 is called an S corporation/S Corp; this structure is designated Subchapter S. S-Corp are unique separate entities from their owners, therefore limiting the level of liability for its shareholders (owners).

With S Corporations, profits and losses are passed through to the owners who file individual tax returns. Any shareholder who is also an employee is required to pay themselves reasonable compensation or the IRS will reclassify the corporate earnings as wage earnings.

To form an S corporation, first the business must file as a corporation. Once all owners agree to the election of becoming an S Corporation, the business should register and like all businesses-obtain licenses and permits. A Limited Liability company wanting to become an S Corp for tax purposes, must file Form 2553 with the IRS within 75 days of the beginning of the tax year the election is to be effective.

Among the advantages of the S Corp structure is: domestic corporations avoid being taxed twice; there are business expense tax credits and other tax savings; and this structure is independent of its shareholders in the event one leaves the company, so that business can continue with little disruption.

S Corporations have a requirement for shareholder compensation which may be seen as a disadvantage; additionally S Corps have strict procedures requiring them to schedule meetings, minutes, by-laws etc.

Register Your Business

The following chapters will give some insight on registering your business. You will want to register as a means of protecting the intellectual property of the business. It gives you the opportunity to claim your right to use a mark; license the use of content and products to others; and ultimately increase the value of your brand.

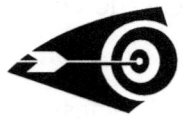

Choose Your Business Name

Experts say choosing a business name is the most important thing to creating a brand; this is true! You should put some thought into creating a name, it's like naming a child for the rest of their life, you need to be thoughtful as you create your brand; but also just so others including yourself know what to call it. There's no need to spend months on it. For the purpose of setting up the business- just choose a name!

If you choose to operate under a name different than your own, then you need to file a fictitious name- otherwise known as the assumed name, trade name, or Doing Business As- DBA. The business name should be unique and original; it cannot be claimed by another business in the same industry.

Suppose your business structure was an LLC, then the name must be different from an existing LLC in your state, it must clearly state that it's an LLC -example "LLC" or Limited Company. A huge tip to consider is whether the name has an available domain name on the web. Also think about how the name will appear on a logo on social media and carefully examine its uniqueness. Do a quick web search to find out if the business name already exists.

There are many free online websites that offer logo designs for your small business should you choose to do it yourself, or you can pay a professional. Make sure that the design which is the mark you will use to identify the business is not infringing on the rights of others, therefore it is a great idea to check with the U.S. Patent & Trademark Office just to see if there are similar names, designs or variations already trademarked. It will cost you approximately $300 to apply for Trademark Protection. If your business name has been previously registered by another business, you might be permitted to still go ahead and claim the proposed name if your company offers different good and services from the listed business and is in a different region.

Register Your Business Name

The name you choose as your business name will automatically be registered with your state once you register your business, so there is little need to go through another channel.

Register With State Agencies

Sole proprietors do not need to register with State government, however, corporations, LLC's and non-profits do. All businesses need to obtain the necessary licenses and permits before they can start operation. Regulations may vary depending on the industry, state and locality of the business.

B.U.S.I.N.E.S.S

ᙠᑌᔕᴉᴎƎᔕᔕ

Alabama, Alaska, Arizona, Arkansas, California, Colorado, Connecticut, Delaware, District of Columbia, Florida, Georgia, Guam, Hawaii, Idaho, Illinois, Indiana, Iowa, Kansas, Kentucky, Louisiana, Maine, Maryland, Massachusetts, Michigan, Minnesota, Mississippi, Missouri, Montana, Nebraska, Nevada, New Hampshire, New Jersey, New Mexico, New York, North Carolina, North Dakota, Ohio, Oklahoma, Oregon, Pennsylvania, Puerto Rico, Rhode Island, South Carolina, South Dakota, Tennessee, Texas, U.S. Virgin Islands, Utah, Vermont, Virginia, Washington, West Virginia, Wisconsin, Wyoming.

Federal Licenses & Permits

Federal Licenses and permits are needed if the business is involved in the following industries:

Transportation and Logistics

Radio and Television Broadcasting

Nuclear Energy

Mining & Drilling

Maritime Transportation

Commercial Fisheries

Fish and Wildlife

Firearms & Explosives

Aviation

Alcohol

Agriculture

Employer Identification Number

Once your business is registered and you have obtained the necessary permits and licenses you are allowed to officially start business. Starting a business can be very rewarding yet overwhelming at times; you may need to hire additional staff with the expertise you need for your business. To apply for an employer ID number, simply visit the IRS website.

Banking & Insurance

It is important to keep good records detailing the transactions of the business; therefore having a separate bank account for your business is important. When choosing a financial institution, you should go with a credit union over banks as they represent the interests of their members. Also, you will find that with credit unions, the fees which take away from your profit will be minimal as compared to banks.

In most cases the following documentation will be needed to open a business account.

Sole Proprietorship (Two (2) forms of identification)
Business License
Fictitious Name Certificate (OR Certificate of Assumed Name)
Federal Tax ID Number (TIN) Letter
Valid Driver's License/Government-Issued Identification

Partnership (All, if applicable)
Partnership Agreement
Federal Tax ID Number (TIN) Letter
Certificate of Good Standing
Fictitious Name Certificate (OR Certificate of Assumed Name)
Business License
Certificate of Limited Partnership
Partnership Authority

Corporation (All if applicable)

Articles of Incorporation
Corporate Bylaws
Certificate of Good Standing
Federal Tax ID Number (TIN) Letter
Certificate of Incorporation or Certificate of Assumed Name

Sole-Member Limited Liability Company (LLC) (All, if applicable)

Articles of Organization
Federal Tax ID Number (TIN) Letter
Certificate of Good Standing
Fictitious Name Certificate or Certificate of Assumed Name
Business License
Operating Agreement

Multi-Member Limited Liability Company (LLC) (All, if applicable)

Articles of Organization
Operating Agreement
Federal Tax ID Number (TIN) Letter
Certificate of Good Standing
Fictitious Name Certificate or Certificate of Assumed Name
Business License

Insure Your Business

Business insurance protects your investment by minimizing financial risks. Some of the unforeseen instances may involve the unexpected death of a partner, a hurt employee, a pending lawsuit, or hurricane disaster. Business insurance is generally not required by law, but it is good to purchase sufficient insurance to protect your assets.

The state in which the business resides will determine the insurance requirements such as workers' compensation insurance, unemployment insurance, and state disability insurance. If you require a vehicle for your business, then you are required to purchase commercial auto insurance. In addition, you may want to get insurance in case of business interruption from fire or flood.

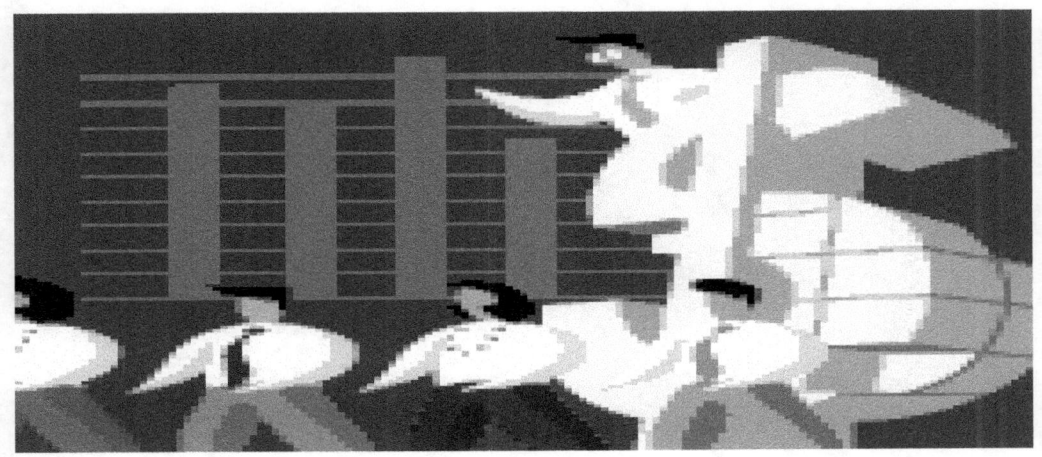

Marketing

There are many forms of advertising to choose from which you will have to bear in mind when focusing in on your target market. You may be required to advertise in the newspaper for certain businesses. TV, Radio & Newspaper contribute to 41% of advertising. Physical direct marketing is the most popular and effective at getting customers to buy. Other options available are online advertising, social media and the yellow pages.

It is a good thing for startups of any type to create an online presence in order to connect with potential customers. Once you have your website created, start to promote your business. Inform the customer of upcoming specials and invite them to sign up for your newsletter to build your loyal fan base.

COMING SOON

Pertrina

Sugar Cakes

Daily specials include:

Pick 3

Buy 1 Get 1 FREE

Flavor of the Month.

Pick Up Menu

Monday	Tuesday	Wednesday	Thursday	Friday	Saturday	Sunday
Chocolate (529calories)	Nut (574calories)	Pineapple-Ginger (317calories)	Trio (505calories)	Cookie (321calories)	*Original (Vegan) (404calories)	CLOSED for pickup

Flavor of the Month

January	February	March	April	May	June
*Original (Vegan) (404calories)	Trio (505calories)	Cookie (321calories)	Pineapple-Ginger (317calories)	Nut (574calories)	Chocclate (529calories)

July	August	September	October	November	December
Apple Cinnamon (320calories)	Rum (505calories)	Chili Pepper (410calories)	Salted Caramel (515calories)	Pumpkin Marshmallow (500calaries)	Chocolate Peppermint (535calories)

Pertrina sugar cakes are individually handcrafted and made from the highest ingredients found in the Caribbean. We place high emphasis on preserving quality of our products. It is recommended for anyone (men, women and children) as an alternative to candy & chocolate, and a replacement for most snack and protein bars.

*The "original" flavor is our best seller, and is suitable for Vegans. We strongly suggest that persons with severe nut allergies avoid consuming our products since under FDA guidelines coconut is classified as a treenut. All our products contain coconut.

Pickups Rules

Pickup orders must be placed at least 24 hours in advance by 3pm. Please select from the menu of flavors available on the day of your planned pickup. Pickup specials are currently 50% off your entire purchase.

Delivery Rules

We offer free delivery to Barbados residents. The minimum order for delivery must be at least $50. All delivery orders must be placed at least 24 hours in advance by 3pm. Please select from the menu of flavors available on the day of your requested delivery. For special delivery including (cards, balloons, flowers) additional charges may apply.

Shipping Rules

We ship internationally to physical addresses within the 50 states. We do not ship to PO boxes or APOs. The minimum order for shipping must be at least $50. Shipping fees are $20 for each item shipped. All orders will be shipped express and will arrive within 3-5 business days with our trusted carriers.

Due to the perishable nature of some products, it is advisable for someone to be present to receive the delivery. Pertrina cannot guarantee delivery if we are provided with an incorrect address, or for shipping delays resulting from inclement weather. You will receive a tracking number via email once your order has shipped.

Catering

Celebrate any occasion with our sugar cakes. We create memorable sugar cakes for that special event in your life (weddings, birthdays, holidays, gifts). For more information or to inquire about special events or large volume orders, please contact our catering team.

Pertrina Community

Share some sugar cakes with friends. Refer-a-friend and receive 50% off the purchase of our books.

We also love hearing from our customers and fans! In addition to following us on Facebook, Instagram, Pinterest and Twitter, check our community page regularly for information on exciting upcoming fundraisers and events.

Send us your favorite pictures of recipes you've created with our sugar cakes and your recipe can be featured in our monthly newsletter. Winner of the featured recipe will receive a FREE product. No purchase necessary.

Help

Orders:

Do I need to order in advance?

Pertrina currently offers 50% off all pickup orders made in advance. Walk-ins are welcome, however only sugar cakes available from our menu on that day will be available. If you request a different flavor you will be charged the retail price.

Can I phone or email an order for pickup?

Yes! We encourage all our customers to order online, however you can call or email your order for pickup ahead of time and receive a confirmation number. We are happy to serve you!

Do you have same day pickups?

Walk-ins are welcome to order from our daily menu, it is not necessary to call in advance for same day orders. Orders for pickups are required to place orders 24hours in advance, by 3pm the day before.

How do I pay?

We request that all orders be paid for in advance by simply placing your order at our online store. Our delivery drivers do not have the capability to receive payment. We accept all forms of payment from our walk-ins customers.

Can I order a flavor not offered on a specific day?

Currently, it is not possible to order a different flavor from that offered on the same day, however exceptions are made for catering and business gift orders.

Does Pertrina deliver?

Yes! There is FREE delivery to Barbados residents. Minimum order is $50. Please have someone present to accept the order. If no one is available a 'delivery attempt' note will be left and the item returned to the store for you to pickup at your earliest convenience. We never charge a delivery fee.

What are the delivery times?

The earliest delivery is between 10am-11pm. Latest delivery is between 4pm - 7pm.

What are the shipping terms?

Pertrina is international. We ship internationally to physical addresses within the 50 states. We do not ship to PO boxes or APOs. The minimum order for shipping must be at least $50. Shipping fees are $20 for each item shipped. All orders will be shipped express and will arrive within 3-5 business days with our trusted carriers.

Due to the perishable nature of some products, it is advisable for someone to be present to receive the delivery. Pertrina cannot guarantee delivery if we are provided with an incorrect address, or for shipping delays resulting from inclement weather. You will receive a tracking number via email once your order has shipped.

What other products does Pertrina sell?

In addition to sugar cakes, we offer specialized popcorn favors to our business clients as well as gourmet coconut bread as part of our catering and gifts package.

How to store our products?

Pertrina products are made to order. Once our sugar cakes packaging is opened the product usually last up to a month if stored in an air tight container. Our unopened products have a shelf life of up to 1 year unless specified on the packaging.

Business Gifts:

Does Pertrina offer discounts for large volume orders?

Yes! Orders of $500 or more receive a %10 discount. In addition we offer free 3-5 day shipping.

Can I customize with my company logo?

Certainly, if you send us your JPEG image company logo, we will customize the packaging for your order. You will receive a confirmation number. Processing time takes 3 weeks. You will be notified once shipped and given a tracking number.

Catering:

Does Pertrina cater for weddings, baby showers, birthdays, holiday and other events?

Let us help make your special day memorable. We offer custom flavors with design upon request.

Is on-site set up included?

Absolutely, we offer on-site set up to Barbados residents. International on-site set up is currently not available. Call our customer care line to speak with an agent to arrange catering for your big event. Also learn of our rates.

Is there individual wrapping?

Yes! Individual wrapping for favors are $5 per favor including customized messaging. Gift wrapping services are available for an additional $5. Please allow 3 weeks for processing.

Does Pertrina offer discounts for large volume catering orders?

Yes! Orders of $500 or more receive a %10 discount in addition to free express shipping (3-5days).

Nutritional Facts:

Are your products gluten-free; vegan or sugar-free?

It is important to note that Pertrina products are not an allergen free. Our main ingredient is coconut. We advise customers with gluten or dairy allergies to be mindful of this if consuming our products.

If I have a nut allergy, should I consume Pertrina sugar cakes?

Pertrina products are not nut-free as our main ingredient is coconut. We advise customers with nut allergies to be mindful of this if consuming our products.

Flavors:

What seasonal flavors do you carry?

Our seasonal flavors are:

July	August	September	October	November	December
Apple Cinnamon (320calories)	Rum (505calories)	Chili Pepper (410calories)	Salted Caramel (515calories)	Pumpkin Marshmallow (500calaries)	Chocolate Peppermint (535calories)

Can I request a personalized/new flavor?

We offer custom flavor as part of our catering package.

Other Questions:

How can I make donations?

We are dedicated to helping the homeless. $1 of every sale made will be donated to "Operation End Homelessness".

What employment opportunities are available at Pertrina?

Periodically, we will post jobs as they become available. We reserve the right to evaluate the skills, knowledge and abilities of each applicant to meet the needs of the company. We are an equal opportunity employer with preference to veterans.

How can I follow Pertrina on social media?

Stay connected with Pertrina, LLC on all of our social media channels:

Twitter: twitter.com/pertrinasugar
Instagram: instagram.com/pertrinasugar
Pinterest: pinterest.com/pertrinasugar

Additional Resources

www.grant.gov

www.irs.gov

www.uspto.gov

www.business.usa.gov

www.gs1us.org

www.tsp.gov

www.dodtap.mil

www.benefits.gov

www.ebenefits.va.gov

www.va.gov

Copyright © 2015 PERTRINA, LLC. All rights reserved.

www.ingramcontent.com/pod-product-compliance
Lightning Source LLC
Chambersburg PA
CBHW071016180526
45168CB00003B/1446